# MOLLY'S
## ORGANIC FARM

By Carol L. Malnor and Trina L. Hunner ❦ Illustrated by Trina L. Hunner

DAWN PUBLICATIONS

**This book is based on the true story of Molly, a little homeless cat who charmed the hearts of everyone she met.**

With gratitude to the many organic farmers who grow healthy and delicious food. — CLM

For the soil, the critters, and everyone who supports organic farming—and for Molly. — TLH

Library of Congress Cataloging-in-Publication Data
Hunner, Trina L.
 Molly's organic farm / by Trina L. Hunner and Carol L. Malnor ;
illustrated by Trina L. Hunner. -- 1st ed.
    p. cm.
 Based on a true story.
 Summary: Wandering into a community organic farm, a homeless cat is
adopted by the farmers and helps out in her own way. End notes discuss
organic farming and present related activities.
 Includes bibliographical resources (p.  ).
 ISBN 978-1-58469-166-2 (hardback) -- ISBN 978-1-58469-167-9 (pbk.)
 [1. Organic farming--Fiction. 2. Farms--Fiction. 3. Cats--Fiction.]  I. Malnor,
Carol. II. Title.
 PZ7.H9113Mo 2012
 [E]--dc23

                                                    2011030890

Book design and production by Patty Arnold, *Menagerie Design & Publishing*

Manufactured by Regent Publishing Services, Hong Kong
Printed January, 2012, in ShenZhen, Guangdong, China

10 9 8 7 6 5 4 3 2 1

First Edition

**Dawn Publications**

12402 Bitney Springs Road
Nevada City, CA 95959
530-274-7775
nature@dawnpub.com

All alone, a homeless cat rambles and roams.

Sometimes she's hungry. Sometimes she's cold.
Each night she searches for somewhere to sleep.

*Whoosh! Creak . . . CRASH!* A gust of wind swings
a gate open and bangs it shut.

A few quick
peeks.
In she streaks.

3

The curious cat looks all around. Stems shoot up. Leaves cover over. Plants spread out.

So much to explore!

Big, brown boots!
Away she scoots.

Farmer's hat
Covers the cat.

From hiding place to hiding place, the stray cat sneaks
down a row when . . . she's discovered!

"Hey, we have a new farmer here!" someone exclaims.
Everyone gathers 'round to greet the new arrival
to the organic farm. "Let's call her Molly."

BEETS

6

Catching whiffs.
Molly sniffs.

A strange scent leads Molly to the compost pile, which is full of plant clippings, pulled-up weeds, and cow manure. Although smelly now, it's *decomposing*—becoming sweet-smelling *compost*. Next year, the farmers will use it to improve the soil. They want healthy soil to grow healthy plants for healthy food.

Molly scampers up to the top of the pile. *Eeew!* Sticky paws! Compost is good for growing plants—not for paws. She gives a disgusted shake.

9

Bees *buzzzzz* and *zzzzzoom* from plant to plant, sipping nectar.

What are those ladybugs up to?
Eating an army of aphids.
And that praying mantis?
Hunting for crickets.

These "helpful" bugs are getting rid of plant pests. Molly has a way to get rid of farm pests too.

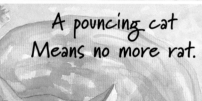

A pouncing cat
Means no more rat.

11

In summer's heat
Molly's beat.

Following a curling cucumber vine, Molly strolls under the sunflowers. *Ahh!* The sunflower's cool shade feels good on a hot afternoon. The cucumbers like it too. Sunflowers and cucumbers are called *companion plants* because they grow best when they're planted next to each other.

Rows of corn tower over Molly. She swipes a silky wisp hanging from a bulging ear of corn—not ripe yet, but soon.

Next year, Molly's farmer friends will plant beans where the corn is growing this year. They'll sow the corn where the beans are growing now. The farmers *rotate* crops to different locations each year to keep the soil and plants healthy.

Corn stalk sways. Molly plays.

Molly yawns a big yawn.
She stretches a big stretch.
While she catnaps, other creatures keep
the farm pest-free. A bird saves a tomato
leaf from a hungry caterpillar, while a frog
searches for bugs on a pepper plant.

Sprinkler starts!
Molly darts.

Farmer's Market day! Produce stands are piled high with colorful fruits and vegetables. What fun! Shoppers meet the local farmers. They fill their bags with organic apples . . . zucchini . . . and everything in between. One of Molly's market-day friends treats her to a bowl of milk. Everyone goes home happy, especially Molly.

Peppers

Radish

Eggplant

Tomatoes

Molly's farm brings the community together. Neighbors chat while kids scramble among the pumpkins.

"My favorite color is orange—just like pumpkins and just like Molly," laughs a little girl. Molly mingles with her friends. She loves her organic farm.

Farm Tour

Harvest Festival

Little girl giggles.
Molly wiggles.

21

An owl nears.
Molly fears.

22

A Harvest Moon rises full and round. Molly crouches low as a bat whizzes overhead. The hissing scream of a barn owl sends her scurrying. But Molly need not be afraid. Nighttime animals are an important part of the balance of life on the farm.

Frost brings a big change to the farm's growing season. "Time to put the farm to bed," the farmers agree. Old stalks and vines are tossed onto the compost pile. A *cover crop* planted in early fall will protect the soil like a blanket during a long winter sleep.

Day by day, Molly sees fewer farmers. Then one day no one comes at all. She shivers.

In the flurries
Molly worries.

Suddenly she feels a warm touch. "Come inside with us," a farmer says, cuddling Molly in her arms. "You'll never need to roam the city streets again. And in the spring you'll be back on the farm with all your friends." Molly purrs.

Safe from harm, Molly dreams of her organic farm.

Beets

27

# READY, SET, GROW!

Organic farmers know that everything that happens on the farm is part of an interconnected system. That's why they use methods that are gentle on nature. They create a healthy growing environment by building good soil and naturally controlling pests, diseases, and weeds. No artificial chemicals, fertilizers, or pesticides are used on an organic farm because these things can harm the soil, plants, animals, and people. Read more about the elements of an organic farm below.

## Healthy Soil and Compost *(pages 8-9)*

Healthy soil is full of life—organic matter, insects, earthworms, air, water, and nutrients. Most of the life in the soil is so tiny that you need a microscope to see it. Healthy soil grows healthy crops. Compost is an organic way to keep soil healthy. Farmers make compost by building a pile of vegetable scraps, leaves, ash, manure, grass and weeds. As the vegetation decomposes (rots), the pile heats up, killing weed seeds, bugs, and potential diseases. Farmers turn the pile to keep it loose and to help it decompose. The compost is ready to be added to soil when it is dark brown, moist, and has an earthy smell.

## Beneficial Bugs *(pages 10-11)*

There are many insect pests that destroy crops. But not all bugs are "bad." Ladybugs (ladybird beetles), spiders, ground beetles, and praying mantises are considered "beneficial bugs" because they help farmers to control other bugs. Honey bees, bumble bees, moths and butterflies are also helpful because they pollinate the flowers. If a flower isn't pollinated, it won't produce food. About one third of our food supply depends on insect pollination, most of which is done by honey bees.

## Companion Planting *(pages 12-13)*

Some plants, like cucumbers and sunflowers, grow best when planted next to each other. They're called "companion plants." Cucumbers like to grow next to sunflowers because the tall sunflowers give cucumbers just the right amount of shade from hot afternoon sun. Some companion plants have natural substances in their roots, flowers, and leaves that keep pests away or attract helpful bugs. Many plants develop better flavor or grow better when planted next to a companion plant.

## Crop Rotation *(pages 14-15)*

Crop rotation is one of the ways farmers replace nutrients in the soil. Planting crops in different locations each year discourages pests and diseases and helps balance nutrients in the soil. Some crops, like corn, are "heavy feeders" and take nutrients out of the soil. But other crops like beans and peas are "givers" and put some nutrients into the soil as they grow. Rotating plantings of "feeders" and "givers" to different places around the farm keeps the soil healthy. Crop rotation is also a natural way to control pests that live in the soil.

## Animal Helpers *(pages 16-17 and 22-23)*

Organic farms depend on a variety of animals to help control pests that damage crops. Cats catch animal pests such as mice, rats, and gophers. Toads, frogs, and lizards eat slugs and insects. Snakes prey on mice and other small mammals that eat crops. Some birds, including wrens, swallows, and chickadees, eat harmful insects. Nighttime animals are also an important part of the balance of life on the farm. Owls catch rats, mice, voles, moles, and other rodents. Bats eat insects, catching thousands every night.

## Buying Locally *(pages 18-19)*

The farmers on Molly's organic farm sell their crops locally at a farmer's market. Locally-grown food takes less time to get from farm to table, which means it's likely to be fresher than food that is transported across the country or from around the world. The fresher the food, the better it tastes and the more nutritious it is too. Molly's organic farm is also an example of a new type of farm called a Community Supported Agriculture (CSA) Farm. People buy a "share" of the farm and become "members." Then throughout the growing season, usually once a week, members receive a box of in-season fruits or vegetables.

## Community Connections *(pages 20-21)*

Organic farms can bring a whole community together through a shared interest in growing and eating healthy food in a healthy environment. When everyone feels connected, a spirit of support and togetherness develops. For thousands of years, communities have had festivals to celebrate harvest time. The Harvest Moon is the full moon closest to the autumnal equinox, which occurs around September 22nd in the northern hemisphere.

## City Farms *(pages 26-27)*

Organic farms can be anywhere—even in the city. Community-run, organic farm projects have sprouted up from New York, Chicago and Detroit to Seattle and Los Angeles; and from Toronto, Ontario, to Vancouver, British Columbia, in Canada. City farms vary in size from small plots in the midst of buildings to larger farms that occupy a number of acres.

## Let's Have a Plant Part-y

*Roots, stems, leaves, flowers, fruit,* and *seeds* are the parts of plants. Each part functions in a different way to help plants grow and reproduce.

**ROOTS**—hold the plant in the soil and soak up water and nutrients for the plant to use

**STEMS**—carry water and nutrients from the roots to the leaves

**LEAVES**—take in air and sunlight to make food. This process is called *photosynthesis* (meaning "made with light")

**FLOWERS**—after pollination, a part of a flower becomes a fruit

**FRUITS**—contain seeds

**SEEDS**—grow into new plants

29

## Cycle 'Round the Seasons

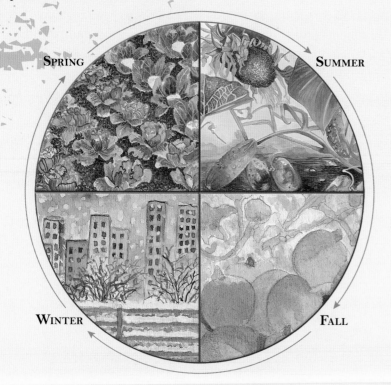

SPRING

SUMMER

WINTER

FALL

In a temperate climate, the life cycle of most plants follows the seasons:

- 🐝 **SPRING:** Seeds are planted and seedlings grow.
- 🐝 **SUMMER:** Plants flower and produce fruit.
- 🐝 **FALL:** Crops are harvested and the farm is put to bed.
- 🐝 **WINTER:** Plants don't grow when the temperature drops below freezing. The farm sleeps.

## Molly's Sense-ational Farm

Molly used her five senses to explore the farm:

  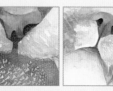

| *eyes* to **see** inside the gate | *ears* to **hear** the owl at night | *paws* to **feel** the sticky compost pile | *tongue* to **taste** a treat at the market | *nose* to **smell** the compost pile |

## Planting Ideas — Growing Creativity

- 🐝 Creative lesson plans and activities specifically for *Molly's Organic Farm* by the authors are available at www.dawnpub.com.
- 🐝 Organic Gardening Resources—http://organicgardening.com
- 🐝 "Take Your Class Outdoors for Organic Gardening," an article about connecting gardening to science standards http://expertvoices.nsdl.org/connectingnews/2010/05/27/take-your-class-outdoors-for-organic-gardening/
- 🐝 Everything you need to know to get started gardening with kids—www.kidsgardening.org
- 🐝 *Roots, Shoots, Buckets & Boots: Gardening Together with Children* by Sharon Lovejoy (Workman, 1999)
- 🐝 *Edible Schoolyard: A Universal Idea* by Alice Waters (Chronicle Books, 2008)
- 🐝 *Smart by Nature: Schooling for Sustainability* by Michael K. Stone, (The Center for Ecoliteracy, 2009)

## Books for Children

- 🐝 *Apple Farmer Annie* by Monica Wellington (Puffin, 2004)
- 🐝 Books about plants by Gail Gibbons (Holiday House): *From Seed to Plant* (1993); *Corn* (2009); *The Pumpkin Book* (2000); *The Vegetables We Eat* (2008)
- 🐝 *Bumpety Bump!* by Pat Hutchins (Greenwillow, 2006)
- 🐝 *Sunflower House* by Eve Bunting (Sandpiper, 1999)
- 🐝 *Jo MacDonald Had a Garden* by Mary Quattlebaum (Dawn Publications, 2012)

- 🐝 **Find out if a pumpkin is a fruit or vegetable.**
- 🐝 **Get a recipe for a "Plant Part-y Salad" you can make with your class.**
- 🐝 **Download a list of all the sensory words used in the story.**

For these and other creative activities and lesson plans, go to www.dawnpub.com, click on "Teachers/Librarians" and "Downloadable Activities."

# The True Story of the REAL Molly

On a cool spring day in 2005, a little orange cat showed up at a small organic farm in the foothills of the Sierra Nevadas in northern California. She was an unusually small cat, probably because she didn't get proper nourishment when she was a kitten. But despite her wild start, she loved to be around people and instantly bonded with the folks at Mountain Bounty Farm. They named her Molly.

As the weather warmed, more and more farmers arrived to work in the fields. Each and every one of them fell in love with her. Molly spent her days frolicking in the chard, zooming through the broccoli, and chasing after all the many farm creatures. In the evenings, she'd curl up on one of the farmer's laps, purring contentedly.

I stopped by Mountain Bounty Farm—one of our local Community Supported Agriculture (CSA) farms—every week during the growing season to pick up a box of organic vegetables, and with each visit I got a special greeting from Molly. I was as excited to see her friendly face as I was to receive my produce.

The summer days passed, fall came, and the farmers began to prepare for winter. Fields were planted with cover crops and tools were packed away. The farmers headed off to other places. But what was to become of Molly? I could almost see the concern on her face as she watched her good friends leave.

My husband and I lived in a small cabin right next to the farm, and we were asked if Molly could spend the winter with us. We jumped at the chance. That first winter was really special. Molly went on long walks with us—even in the snow! In the evening, she spent hours curled up by the fire or snuggled in our laps. And when the first spring crops began to sprout, Molly headed back to the farm.

So it was for four seasons—Molly socializing at the farm in spring and summer, then spending a quiet fall and winter with us. This book is written in loving memory of Molly, a homeless cat that found not one but two homes.

~ Trina L. Hunner

31

CAROL L. MALNOR discovered the joys of organic gardening while living in northern Michigan. Currently, she's a member of a CSA and grows a bumper crop of tomatoes in the foothills of California's Sierra Nevada. Carol focuses on her favorite environmental topics as she writes for a wide variety of audiences. In *The BLUES Go Birding* picture books series, Carol shares her passion for birding with a young audience. For older children, she taps into the power of biography through the *Earth Heroes* series. And drawing on 20+ years as a teacher, she authored a series of teacher's guides. She writes a blog, announces her nature workshops, and has numerous recommendations for teachers and parents on her website, www.naturebooksforkids.com.

TRINA L. HUNNER loves to eat organic fruits and vegetables, especially kale. For several years she lived adjacent to an organic community farm near Nevada City, California. She and her husband Nikos began to "mark our lives around the cycles and rituals of the farm." She even spent a few spring days planting with the farmers and developed an immense respect for them and the hard work farming takes. The quality of the food itself convinced her that healthy, fresh food has transformative powers and made her passionate about eating and promoting local, organic foods. She can often be found riding her bike to the elementary school where she teaches, skiing in the mountains near her home, or cuddling her cat Charlotte.

Dawn Publications is dedicated to inspiring in children a deeper understanding and appreciation for all life on Earth. You can browse through our titles, download resources for teachers, and order at www.dawnpub.com or call 800-545-7475.

## Other Children's Books by Carol L. Malnor

*The BLUES Go Birding Across America, The BLUES Go Birding At Wild America's Shores,* and *The BLUES Go Extreme Birding* — Three books that introduce birds to young children. The information is accurate and useful for a young birder, and presented with a generous helping of humor.

*Earth Heroes: Champions of the Wilderness* and *Earth Heroes: Champions of Wild Animals* — Each of these books for middle school children presents the biographies of eight of the world's greatest naturalists, with special attention not only to their careers and lasting contributions, but also to events in their youth that foreshadowed greatness.

## SOME OTHER BOOKS FROM DAWN PUBLICATIONS

The **"Mini-Habitat" Series** — Beginning with the insects to be found under a rock (*Under One Rock: Bugs, Slugs and Other Ughs*) and moving on to other small habitats (around old logs, on flowers, cattails, cactuses, and in a tidepool), author Anthony Fredericks has a flair for introducing children to interesting "neighborhoods" of creatures. Field trips between covers! Check out all of the Mini-Habitat series titles at http://www.dawnpub.com/our-store/habitats/.

The **"Over" Series** — Kids sing, clap, and think these books are entertainment while adults think they are educational! Patterned on the classic old tune of "Over in the Meadow," this series by Marianne Berkes includes *Over in the Ocean, Over in the Jungle, Over in the Arctic, Over in the Forest,* and *Over in Australia.*

*Jo MacDonald Had a Garden* and *Jo MacDonald Saw a Pond* are delightful gardener's (and nature-lover's) variations on "Old MacDonald Had a Farm." Jo is Old MacDonald's granddaughter and his farm is such a cool place. E—I—E—I—O!

*In the Trees, Honey Bees* offers an inside-the-hive view of a wild colony, along with solid information about these remarkable and valuable creatures.